Inner Wisdom

Tough it may be, yes we ~~~~~
Quit puttin~ ~~~~~~~~~~~~~~~~~~~~~~~
For in the ~~~~~~~~~~~~~~~~~~~~~~~
Ex~ ~~~~~~~~~~~~~~~~~~~~~~~

Hold your h~ ~~~~~~~~~~~~~~~~~~~
That's where ~~~~~~~~~~~ss possibilities start

When you see with your eyes it all seems to lack
But when you see with your heart you'll take it all
back

The eyes are with limits that keep yourself stuck
Worrying and fearing that there's never enough

Let your heart open and feel what's inside
For what you will find is eternal and kind
When the doors of love open you will find
That what has been missing was always inside

Julie Nichol

ABOUT THE AUTHOR

Julie has been working with the concepts taught in Pathway to Prosperity for more than 8 yrs. She started her journey into the metaphysical world after her 18 yr old brother was tragically killed in a car accident. As a single mother of two young boys, living in low income housing and working two jobs, she knew that there had to be a better life available for her. She began learning feng shui; this alone changed her life. She bought her own home (just a little fixer upper) and opened an in-home day care. Her day care flourished with the use of feng shui principals and she had to hire her sister to help her. She eventually out grew the little house and purchased a middle class home in a well-to-do area and reestablished her day care there. Over time the day care was no longer satisfying and she needed something more. Julie knew that feng shui was very powerful and helped bring her to this point but there was something missing. That's when she started meditating, and at-tending science of mind classes. She learned the power of her thoughts. After regular practice of meditating every day Julie started receiving messages from her brother that had passed away as well as her spirit guide Nazura.

They were guidng her life. Suddenly she understood things that were beyond her knowledge. Julie always had friends that did not have a lot of money or happiness. They would always come to her and ask what they should do about certain situations in there life. The spirit guides would always have an answer. This information was not only changing her life but the life of those around her. That's when she decided to write Pathway to Prosperity to help other to change their lives. All of the information in this book has come from her studies or been channeled from higher consciousness. It is amazing how powerful this information is when you apply it to your life.

Pathway to Prosperity
by Julie Nichol

Table of Contents

INTRODUCTION

Everything that you do, say, and think has an energy to it. Energy runs in and through all things. When we can get all of our thoughts, feelings, actions, beliefs, and even our environment energetically working with us and not against us we can create our lives just as we want them to be.

This book has been designed to bring you the most abundant life possible. In this program, you will learn about how you keep yourself from having the prosperous life that you deserve. You will learn about what you do subconsciously that keeps you from the life of your dreams. You may even learn to identify what your dream life looks like!

I have taken my life experience, along with my *feng shui* knowledge and the information I receive from guidance, and put it all in this program. The purpose of the program is to help you achieve the life you have always wanted and to start to notice the things that keep you from your ideals. You can intend and you can believe, but if you are contradicting your intentions and beliefs with your feelings, actions, and environment, then you are contradicting yourself. You are keeping yourself stuck—holding yourself just short of your goals.

YOUR LIMITING BELIEFS

First, let's talk about beliefs. What you believe about money has a *huge* effect on how it shows up for you. Here are some beliefs that can hold you back from having the prosperity you desire.

1. The first common limiting belief is the idea that you have to work hard for money. This belief itself can *keep* you having to work hard for money. Money is an energy field that you need only to draw to you. The sooner you let go of the belief of having to work hard for money, the sooner you can start drawing it to you easily.

2. Another limiting belief is the idea

that there is not enough to go around. This is a belief in lack. Sometimes the thought shows up as: "I'd better get while the getting is good." Or, it might show up as: "I better get my piece of the pie." With these thoughts, you are affirming that there is not enough for everyone and also enough for you. Therefore, you are sending out signals to the universe that say, "there is not enough for everyone!" So, lack is what shows up for you.

3. Another belief is the idea that money is hard to come by. Perhaps you believe that money doesn't come easily and effortlessly. If so, you are setting yourself up to have to struggle to get it. Money is energy field. All you need to do to have it is match your vibration to it.

4. You might also limit yourself by believing that there is no such thing as "easy money." This is a belief that will keep you having to work hard for the rest of your life. Money is an energy field. You can't draw it to yourself from the outside-in. Instead, you must draw it to yourself from the inside-out.

To do so, you must release your emotional attachments to it. Being emotionally attached to money keeps it from flowing freely. It is okay to like money; it is even OK to want lots of it. Keeping it from flowing is like damming water. The water becomes stagnant and cannot flow.

5. Another limiting belief is the idea that money can only come from a job. If you believe that the only way to make money is from a job, you are holding yourself back from the *endless possible ways in which it might come to you*. Sure, you have been taught that the only way to make money is from a job. You can shift that belief to knowing that money can come in unexpected and abundant ways. Then you will start opening the doors for more of it to come to you. Instead of thinking of money as coming from just one source, focus on creating *many* avenues for money to come to you.

6. You can also hold yourself back by believing that if you achieve money easily, then there is a "higher price" to pay. This is a belief in a life of limitations and punishment. If you achieve money easily, it is because you're drawing it to you. There is no negative consequence for that!

7. Some of you may believe that

there is such a place as the poor house. There is no such place as the poor house. So, take that phrase out of your vocabulary! This belief suggests that we do *not* live in a limitless universe and you are *not* provided for at all times. In reality, no matter what the situation looks like, you *are* provided for at all times. When you can get clear on that, you are moving with the universe—not against it.

8. Road blocks can also come from believing that "there isn't going to be enough for you when you get there." We live in an abundant and limitless universe. It is *always* providing us with everything we need. Know that there is always enough for you.

9. Perhaps you believe that you can't make money doing what you love. If you have a hobby or a passion, follow it. Know that you can always make money doing what you love. This is because when you love what you do, you can only draw good to you. Pursue the work that you are passionate about.

10. A further limiting belief is the idea that others are more deserving than you. If you always give to others and never take for yourself, you are sending signals to the universe that say "I do not deserve this good. Please give my share to someone else." Although giving is always wonderful, there has to be a balance. You have to fill yourself up, too.

11. You block prosperity by believing you are not good enough to have what you want. For instance, you might walk into someone else's home or environment and notice that the surroundings are what you would consider "nicer" or "more expensive" than your own. You might feel that you do not belong in these nicer surroundings. When you feel that, you are sending out signals that you are not good enough to have those things for yourself.

12. A big limitation occurs when you assume that those who have money did not come about it honestly. This assumption sends out a signal that people must lie or steal to have wealth. You will keep abundance from you with this belief. It's like saying, "the only way to have money is to lie and steal. And, since I am an honest person, I will be poor forever."

13. Finally, one huge limiting idea is the notion that if you didn't graduate high school or go to college, you are doomed to a life of poverty. This is a false belief! If you believe in yourself, you can accomplish anything!

To assume that a classroom environment, and therefore a college degree, is for everyone is nonsense. We are here as spiritual beings to teach and learn unconditional love for one another, and to enjoy the journey of doing so. *Your only purpose here on this planet is to find what brings you joy and love and to live a limitless life on your journey.* What would make a person think that college is meant for everyone, that studying textbooks is what makes everyone on the planet happy, and that work you love can only be obtained if you have a college degree?

I am not saying that you shouldn't go to college. Certainly you *can* go to college, study a certain subject, and get a career in that line of work that may pay well. However, if that path doesn't appeal to you, know that there are a million ways to make money *without* a college education. It was Einstein himself who said, "Imagination is more important than knowledge." Find what you love, what brings you joy, and follow that. That is where your true success lies. When you love what you do, only good can come to you.

A PROGRAM FOR CHANGE

Step One: Empowering Affirmations

These can be deep-seated beliefs that you have believed your whole life. What can you do to start shifting these beliefs and changing your life? One of the simplest things to do is to start working with affirmations. Affirmations are positive statements that reflect beliefs you do want to have. Post them around your house and say or read them as often as possible. Bring a copy in your car and say them at red lights. Every time it crosses your mind, say your affirmations until they start to become a part of your vocabulary.

Here are some examples of affirmations you might use:

- Money is an energy field that flows in great abundance.

- Money is easy to come by.
- I live in a limitless universe that always supplies all of my needs.
- Abundance is my life.
- Money comes to me with ease.
- I deserve to be abundant.
- I live in a universe that always provides for every person and animal, including me.
- I love my work, and it brings me great prosperity.

Step Two: Aligning Your Environment

In addition to working with affirmations, you might also increase your abundance by shifting your environment. Everything that you place in or around your environment has a direct effect on your life. It may be that you have set an intention for something and you have been thinking positive thoughts, but your environment is actually contradicting you. This makes it more difficult for your intention to manifest in your reality. In this section, I will give you some basic *feng shui* tips to use to start getting your environment to work for you and not against you. Using the ancient Chinese principles of *feng shui*, we draw energy to our environment and keep it moving in harmony with us—not too fast or too slow.

The Path to Your Door

Let's start with the front of your house. Especially if you are on a corner or a cul-de-sac, you will benefit from putting a pinwheel or a gazing ball out in your yard. This will help to slow down any attacking energy. The movement of the pinwheel will attract energy to you.

The address of your home should be clearly posted where it can easily be seen. Why? Because if people can't find your home, how can energy? You should also be able to see the entrance to your home from the road. If not, the path to your front door should be obvious. Make a well-lit path, free from clutter and debris. Line the walkway to the door with plants or other decorative items—anything to draw the eye and therefore energy to the front door. If you have shrubs that protrude into the walkway, trim them back. You do not want your visitors to feel like they are being attacked as they approach your home.

If there are stairs leading up to your front door, they should be wide and shallow. Steeper stairs require planters on them, or light that shines upward on them, to lift the energy to the door. Flowerpots with brightly colored flowers work well here. The flowers should be living. In winter months, you may want to consider placing artificial flowers in your pots. Artificial flowers work better than dead flowers, because dead flower are dead energy. Set the flowers on the steps to draw the energy up.

If the steps to your door are wooden steps with open backs, so you can see in between each step, enclose the steps. These gaps are allowing energy to leak and fall back down, so it never reaches your front door. In order to have the energy flowing effectively in your home, you first need to get it in the door! Painting the door a bright color such as red will help draw the energy to the door.

Your Entryway

Once we have arrived at your front door, the door should open freely. There should be nothing behind the door, allowing it to open only partially. If your door cannot open all the way, how is the entire energy going to come in? If it is blocked from opening freely, only partial energy will enter. On the inside of the door, your entryway should also be free from debris. It should feel open when people enter the environment.

Some people's entryways are set up so that the energy rushes out of the back of the house or up or down stairs. This requires what we call a cure. First, stand at the front door, looking inside your home. If you can see straight out a back window or door, hang a crystal at least 50 millimeters in diameter in between the front door and the back door or window. The crystal will keep the energy that you just got in the front door from rushing right out the back of the house. You worked so hard to get the energy in—now let's keep it in!

If when the front door is open, the first thing you see is a stairway leading up or down, you can be assured that the energy is either rushing from upstairs down at you, or rushing down into the basement, or sometimes both. If your stairs go up, hang a crystal at the top of the stairs to slow the energy down. Place some decorative art, plants, or lights on the stairway wall without blocking the walkway, or even weave vines between the rails. This will draw the attention upward. If the stairs lead down, again hang a crystal at the top of the staircase to slow down the energy. If there is a door to these stairs, keep it closed. Place a planter or art on the wall to draw the energy into the home. The item should be placed on the side of the stairs that heads into the house—not on the side that leads downstairs.

Clearing Clutter

Now that we are in your home and past the attacking and draining energy of the stairs, we can talk about what is in your home that might be keeping your prosperity from you. The number one thing that people have in their homes that keeps them from prospering is clutter.

I know you have all heard, "clear the clutter." But did you ever know why? Clutter sends a message to the universe that says, "We have too much here—please do not bring us any more. We do not have room for it!" In addition to conveying this message, clutter slows energy down and even stops it from moving.

Think of a river, and imagine that the water in the river is the energy flowing in your home. The sticks and rocks in the riverbed are like the clutter in your environment. If there are too many sticks and rocks in the riverbed, they stop the flow of the water. The water then becomes stagnant. This is *exactly* how clutter affects your life. It slows your life energy down so that the energy becomes stagnant, and your life becomes stuck. If you ever feel like you are spinning your wheels and cannot get going, check your environment for clutter.

Broken, Unwanted, and Dead Objects

Three particularly draining types of clutter are broken objects, unwanted items, and anything dead in your home. Fix anything that is broken. I do not care if it is a leaky faucet or a broken toy, if it is broken, either fix it or get rid of it. Hanging on to a broken item and not repairing it tells the universe that either you cannot afford to buy a new item, or you do not deserve a new one. This is poverty-minded behavior. If it can't be fixed, out it goes. Do not put off fixing things, either—this is just you subconsciously keeping yourself stuck.

Get rid of unwanted items, too. Only put things in your environment that bring you joy. Having things in your home that do not bring you joy gives a clear message to the universe. This message is: "I do not deserve the things that do bring me joy, so I will put this in here because I do not deserve to have what I want." I do not care who bought the item for you, who gave it to you, or how much you spent on it. If you do not like it, out it goes. When you feel good about the things in your environment, you feel good about your environment. Your environment is then a much happier place to be.

Finally, do not keep anything dead in your home. This includes dried flowers. Dead items are dead energy, which cannot benefit your life because it's dead.

Kitchens and Bathrooms

When it comes to abundance, two special rooms in your home are the kitchen and the bathroom. The kitchen is particularly important because of the stove. In *feng shui*, no matter where in the home the stove is located, it always represents prosperity. You should keep your stove clean and use it at least once a day, even if only to boil water. Also, placing a mirror behind the stove magnifies it and therefore multiplies your prosperity. Having a mirror behind the stove assures you that you can always see what's behind you, therefore eliminating unexpected encounters. Also, it magnifies the food you are cooking, sending a message of abundance. And while you're in the kitchen area, place a bowl of fruit on the table. This lets the universe know that there is always plenty for everyone.

Bathrooms contain a lot of drains, and they therefore drain energy. To prevent your energy from going down the drain, keep all toilet lids closed. Keep the bathroom door closed as well.

Your Prosperity Corner

Now that we've covered kitchens and bathrooms, let's look also at a special part of your home that relates to prosperity. This is known as your prosperity corner.

To find your prosperity corner, you'll need to use one of the most powerful tools of *feng shui*: the bagua map. The bagua map is made of nine different sections. In *feng shui*, these sections are called "guas," so the whole map is called the bagua. Each section on the bagua represents a different area of your home, which corresponds to a specific area of your life. I have included a bagua map in the back of this book. Before you read further you may want to locate it and review it with me.

To line up your bagua map, stand at your front door, facing inside the home. Your front door corresponds with the bottom line of your bagua map. When we use the bagua, we always work from the main floor of the home. So, from the front door facing in, go to the farthest left corner of your home. Don't just go to the farthest left corner of the room, but the farthest left corner of your entire house. This corner is the prosperity corner of your home.

Everything in here should make you feel rich and abundant. Good colors for this room are purple, gold, red, and green. If this room is a bathroom, it should be energized with bright colors because of all the drains and draining energy. If this room is the laundry room, again energize it with bright colors. If it is a bedroom, go with more relaxing colors—purple or green or even brown are okay here.

If this room is a family or living room, make sure that the furniture makes you feel good and rich. One idea is to place a plant here with leaves that move in an upward direction, such as bamboo. This helps lift the energy and raise the vibration of the room. If you do place a plant here, however, make sure that it is living and has no dying leaves. The plant needs to be alive and healthy, so that your wealth is alive and healthy!

If your prosperity corner is your kitchen, do not over-energize this room, because a kitchen with all of the appliances already has a lot of energy. Never paint a kitchen red. Red represents fire energy. Since the kitchen already has a lot of energy anyway, you will find yourself being angry and arguing a lot in a red kitchen. But if your kitchen is in your prosperity corner, ground it with browns and green. This will balance its overwhelming energy.

A water feature is good in your prosperity corner also. This is true as long as your prosperity corner is <u>not</u> in your bedroom. If you decide to put a water feature in your prosperity corner, make sure it is in good working order. Water always represents prosperity, so if you place a water feature here, it needs to work and be used daily. If you do not wish to maintain a water feature, how about a nice picture of some water that is moving gently, like a river? Make sure that the picture makes you feel good and is not rushing like an aggressive waterfall. Remember that water in the bedroom is not a good thing, so if your bedroom is your prosperity corner, avoid the water. Instead, you can use color here, or even choose furniture and bedding that make you feel rich.

Don't Forget the Yard!

Now let's go out into the yard. Like your house, your yard has a prosperity corner as well. It's important to give that some attention, too.

To find the prosperity corner of your yard, use your bagua map. Start wherever you enter the yard. Line up your bagua map, and look for the farthest left corner of the yard, facing into the yard from where you entered. This is your yard's prosperity corner. The best thing to have here would be a fruit tree, because fruit trees nourish you and produce in great abundance. Also great here are bright flowers. Keep the prosperity colors of purple, gold, red, and green in mind—although any color is good. Any kind of plants, trees, or bushes will work, too. This is a great place for a water feature as well. Just make sure the water flows toward the house.

Again, whatever you place here should be in good working order. It should be alive and healthy, and it should make you feel good. Broken things here say, "broken prosperity." Dead things here again are dead energy. How can you manifest prosperity with dead or broken things in your prosperity corner?

You should definitely have something in this part of your yard, because you do not want this area empty. An empty prosperity area signals empty energy, which means an empty pocket book! If planting something here is not an option, how about a wind chime? Wind chimes have two of the *feng shui* cures: sound and movement. Even a bird feeder would work—wildlife always promotes prosperity. Another idea is a windsock. With that, at least you will have some brightly colored movement. Remember that we always need to keep the energy moving in and around our environment in order to get it working with us.

Step Three: Your Thoughts and Speech

So, you've analyzed your beliefs, and you're doing your affirmations, and you've got your environment working for you. Yet, the money still doesn't appear to be flowing. What else could you possibly need to change? What about what you are thinking and speaking?

Everything you are thinking and speaking, you are creating. Why? Because everything is energy. *Everything* you think and say is creating your reality. So, what are you thinking to yourself? What are you saying to your friends and family?

Invitations

Here's an example that might be familiar. Your friend calls you and says, "hey, let's go to lunch!" Payday isn't until next week, and you are on your last dollar. You know that you do not have enough money for lunch, so what do you do? Telling your friend, "I can't afford lunch" will only create *more* of not being able to afford lunch. So, what do you say instead? Tell your friend, "My current situation doesn't allow for that. How about if we go to lunch next week?" This reply is *not* saying that you do not have the money. It is also not saying that you don't have the time. It is simply saying that you are not able to go to lunch at the moment, but you are scheduling another time.

Now, chances are that while you are saying this to your friend, you are thinking about how much money you do not have. So, while you are responding to your friend, you need to switch your thinking to pure abundance. If you need to close your eyes and see an abundance of money in your mind, do so. Feel the money flowing to you as you say to your friend, "I am sorry, but my current situation does not allow for that right now. How about if we go next week?"

Let's say that your current situation is that you live paycheck to paycheck, and you do not know when you will be able to afford lunch. Say, "I'm sorry; I'm going to have to take a rain check. Can I call you when that might me more doable? " Leave the invitation open to reschedule for another day, but do not set the exact date. Never tell your friend, "I can't afford it." Or "well, I'd like to, but I have no money." If you do, that is what you will create more of.

While you are telling your friend, "I'm sorry; I'm going to have to take a rain check," be thinking about how rich and abundant you are. Visualize it; feel as if you are rich and abundant. If you are speaking one thing and thinking another, you are actually creating the situation that you have the most feeling toward. So, as you turn down the invite, make sure that your mind is focused on abundance.

Shopping for Clothes

Next, you walk into a store, and you are buying a new pair of pants. You only have $20 in your budget. You look around and finally you find the perfect pair. You look at the price tag, and the pants are $35.00. Immediately you think, "Thirty five dollars—I can't afford that," and you start to feel bad about your financial situation. You have to stop in that moment and shift your thinking to absolute prosperity. Visualize yourself in that moment being able to afford whatever you want. Know that you are an abundant creation. Do not let the thoughts and feelings of not having enough money take over. Focus on pure abundance and know that that is your natural state of being.

Whenever the thoughts of "I cannot afford that" come about, shift your thinking to knowing the truth of who you are. That is *pure abundance*. Let your knowing overpower the doubts. Do not let your knowing of your abundance stop with just a pair of pants. Let it apply to *everything* in your life. This goes for houses, cars, vacations—whatever you think you cannot afford. Let your thoughts of pure abundance overpower the thought of "I can't afford that!"

Then buy the pair of pants you can afford. Hold the vibration of absolute prosperity. Thank the universe for bringing you the money to afford those pants. The same can be said for everything else. If, in that moment, you really need to have a car and you can only afford the one that is just okay, thank the universe for the money you do have. Know that there is more coming to you, and that if you only trust and know, the car of your dreams is just around the corner.

Buying Groceries

Here's another example of how your thinking affects your abundance. You walk into a grocery store, and you are having a sudden craving for a nice juicy steak. You planned on spending about $20 on your total dinner purchase, and although you have a large bank account consisting of hundreds or thousands of dollars, you have no intention of spending that money. That money is simply your safety net, so it's not like you are on your last dollar.

You get to the meat department, and on your way you've already picked up the potatoes you are going to bake and the ingredients for your salad. At this point, you've already spent $10 of the $20 that you planned on spending. You're standing in the meat department, and there it is: the perfect juicy steak. It looks delicious! You pick it up, and the price tag says $20.00, and you say, "What? I am not spending $20 on a steak!" You look for a cheaper one, and you do not see one, so you buy chicken. No! You just sent out a message to the universe that you do not deserve— nor can you afford—what you really want, so you'll settle for less.

It is not like you couldn't afford to spend an extra $10 on your dinner. You just decided, in that moment, that you didn't deserve it. This will only help you to create lack in your life. You just said in your mind, "even though I have extra money in my bank account, I do not deserve to spend $10 extra dollars on myself, so I will settle for what I do not really want in order to help maintain the security I have in my bank account. The universe is limiting, and therefore I need to hoard money in my account, because there is never going to be enough."

Does this mean you should not save money? No, it simply means that you can save money, but do not sacrifice what you really want in order to save it. This goes for everything in your life, no matter what the cost. *Do not give up what you really want in order to hoard money for a sense of security.*

Your Job

Another thought that holds a lot of people from their prosperity is the idea that if they lose their job, they will lose everything. With this thinking, people tend to keep themselves stuck by staying in jobs they hate. Remember that your *only* job is to enjoy the journey of this life. If you are staying in a job that you hate because you think you need the money, you are not trusting in the power greater than you.

You cannot possibly think that you will benefit from going somewhere where you are completely miserable everyday. You have to know, first of all, that you deserve to work somewhere you love. Next, you have to believe that money comes in abundant ways and that something better is waiting for you. Trust that if you lose your job, that experience is your push to get you to the next level—to help you find a job that brings you happiness and abundance.

See every situation as a stepping stone, even if it looks like something negative to you. You have to know that this situation is the next step to help you to your ultimate destination of joy and happiness. If you start to look at the world with a different set of eyes, you will see the benefit in what you once thought was negative. You will start to see stress and depression dissolve, because you can see from another view. *That* is true prosperity.

Rich People Thinking

If you do not have money, chances are you have come from a family that does not have a lot of money. Because of this, there are certain thoughts you have been taught that are keeping you stuck. When I began this journey seven years ago, I lived in low income housing and therefore not only did *I* think a certain way, but also so did a lot of others who lived around me. We thought such thoughts as "only rich people can do or afford that." Understanding these thoughts is *huge*. The sooner you realize that you are capable of things that you thought only rich people could do, the sooner you start opening doors for you.

I know a lot of people who think that vacations are only for rich people or that housecleaners are something only rich people have. When you put a few dollars aside and know that you can afford these things and deserve them, you will be amazed at how affordable they seem to become. I myself travel a lot as a single mom with two children. We once lived in a very low-income neighborhood and later moved to a middle class neighborhood. In both places, others often asked us, "How do you afford these vacations you go on? Are you rich?" The answer is, "only *you* think that vacations are not affordable. We know they are."

If you set the intention and even a price you have in mind for something, you will be surprised to see the way it will show up. You just have to start knowing that your desires are not something only rich people do or have. They are also things that *you* can do or have.

Step Four: Abundant Actions

Now that we've looked at affirmations, your environment, and your thoughts and speech, let's take a look at a fourth key factor: your actions.

What actions are you taking that might be working against you? Whether or not you know it, what you are doing is helping to create your reality. So, let's talk about things you are doing that might be holding you back from your abundance— and how to change those behaviors.

Clearance Shopping

First, let's talk about clearance shopping. I know there are a lot of you out there who love to "clearance shop." Here is the deal on that. Say you go to the store and you need to get a new dress. When you get there, you find one that you want to purchase, and it happens to be on clearance. That's great! Celebrate, because the universe has just brought you the right dress at a great price.

However, if you are a person who has plenty of clothes, and you really do not need anything, and you go clearance shopping and buy things just because they're a good price, *that* is poverty-minded thinking. It is saying to the universe: "I do not have enough money, nor will I ever have enough money, to afford these things when I need them. I'd better stock up now while I can afford it, because I will not be able to afford it later." This is a belief in lack.

This idea is not true just for clothes. It is true for everything. Those "day-after-Christmas" sales, the "store closing" sales, and the "end-of-season specials" are okay if there is something that you: 1.) need; 2.) will use; 3.) have room for; 4.) know will not be clutter in your home; and 5.) really want—in other words, you are not buying it just because it is a good price. Again, understanding this is huge, because if you are going to clearance sales and just buying for the price, you are keeping yourself stuck.

Clearance shopping gets back to one of the first beliefs we talked about. That is the idea that "You better get while the getting is good. Because there won't be enough later, and there is never enough." If you act based on this belief, then lack is what will show up in your reality. If you take this stuff home and it becomes clutter, that is even worse. Then your energy can't move, either. If you are going to buy something on clearance, think about it first, and make sure you are buying it for the right reasons.

Shopping in Bulk

Okay, now let's talk about shopping in bulk. Shopping in bulk is okay if you will *use* the items you buy in bulk. You should not walk into the store and stock up on a large quantity of an item that you do not even have room for in your home just because the price is right. Sure, you see a good deal, and you might buy a few extra, but to stock up is limited thinking—especially if you do not have enough room in your home to store the items.

Thinking that you have to stock up whenever you see a good price is saying to the universe, "I will not have enough money to buy this product later. I better get all that I can now, because in the future I will not be able to afford these things." So, what do you think your reality will be? Continuing to need to stock up because you will not have enough later!

Impulse Buys

Do you buy things impulsively? Do you go to the store and just throw things in the basket without even thinking about it? This is scattered thinking. It is pushing your good away, because you are not centered and focused on what you do want. Instead, you go to the store not knowing what it is you really want, and you randomly buy. When you get home, you may find that you do not even use whatever it is you just purchased.

One of the keys to prosperity is being clear in your mind about what you want in the first place. Chances are, if you are randomly buying stuff impulsively, you do not have the money in your current reality to purchase things you might really want. If you are going grocery shopping, make a list. If you are going to the mall, know what you are looking for. Be clear that you need it and will use it before your purchase it. It is okay to stray from the list a little, but if you are just acting on impulse, then you are not clear on what you want.

Lying and Stealing

Another action to shift is the "little white lie." Let's say you go to the local amusement park, where the price for an adult is $39.95, and the price for a child is $20.95. An adult is considered to be anyone 12 or older. Well, little Johnny is with you, and he just turned 13. He is a small thirteen, so you say to yourself, "I can pass him off for an eleven-year-old and save myself $19.00."

Even though in that moment, it may look like you are saving yourself a little money, in the big picture of life, you are really costing yourself more money. You just said with that action, "I cannot afford to pay full price. I have to lie to get the things in life that I want." So, lack is what shows up in your reality, because what you stated that you are is limited. How can you possibly expect to manifest an abundance of money if you have to lie to save a few dollars? It doesn't matter if you are lying to save $1 or $1,000, you are still sending a signal to the universe that says "I do not have enough."

What about stealing? I do not care what you steal—whether it is pens and paperclips from the office, or a something major, like a car. If you are taking things that do not belong to you, no matter how small they are, you are telling the universe that the only way you can receive good in your life is by stealing it.

It seems innocent enough: you throw a handful of paper clips in your pocket before leaving work. But, in the mind of the universe, you are sending a message, and believe me, you are paying a high price for those paperclips. You are telling the universe: "I do not have enough to pay for those things myself, so I will just take what is not mine." How can you possibly draw an abundance of money to you when this is what your actions say?

Step Five: Valuing Yourself

Finally, let's talk about self-value. If you are giving away self-value, you cannot draw good to yourself. You are sending a message to the universe that says, "I do not deserve good in my life. Give it to someone else, or just take it far from here, because I do not deserve it." So, what things might you be doing that are giving away your self-value?

1. You do things for your friends, family, and co-workers not because you want to, but because you do not know how to say no. Do not confuse this with giving from an open heart. If you are doing things for others because you want to and because you feel good about it, certainly do as many favors as you would like for these people. But, if your sister calls you to baby sit every Friday night, and when the phone rings you say, "here we go, she wants me to baby sit again," and even though you dread it, you still do not say no—*that* is giving away self-value. You have to learn that it is okay to say no. If you say no when you really do not want to do something, then you will feel good about doing something when you do want to.

2. You allow others to take advantage of you, without setting boundaries for yourself or establishing self-respect. If you are allowing others to take advantage of you, you are sending a message that says, "There is not enough good for me. I'll give away my good so that others can have what I do not deserve." In order for others to respect you, you have to respect yourself.

3. You don't take time for you. You have to be able to fill yourself up before you can afford to fill up others. If you never take time for yourself, and everyone else always comes first, you are saying to the universe that you do not deserve good— only others do. Put some time aside each day for you. Take a hot bath, go for a walk, read a book . . . whatever you like to do. Make sure you do something. If you only give to others and never take for yourself, how can you possibly expect to manifest abundance in your life? You have to be able to receive for you. This does not mean to never give to others. However, there has to be a balance of give and take.

Guidelines

Here are a few guidelines for strengthening your self-value. First, do not compare yourself to others. Instead, know that right where you are is perfection. Visualize yourself where you do want to be. When you compare yourself to others, you put your attention on your insecurities and what you do not have, rather than on the perfection of who you are and the perfection of everyone and everything around you.

Next, do not gossip about what others have or do. If you are talking with your friends in a negative manner about how much Sally down the street spends on groceries or how much she spends on vacations, you are noticing that you do not have those things for yourself. On the other hand, if Sally is in financial hardship, do not gossip about that either. Such gossip reflects a belief in lack and focuses your attention on lack. This only helps you to create lack for yourself. If you must talk about Sally down the street, do it in a positive manner. Feel *excited* for her that she has enough money to do those things.

Envy sends a signal that you notice that you do not have or deserve what others have. This emotion says to the universe that you will never have those things for yourself. When observing what others have that might bring you envious feelings, shift your thoughts to the positive. Think, "This is what I would like to see in my life, and I can acquire it easily." Feel as happy for others for having acquired those things as you would feel for yourself if those things were yours.

Along with avoiding envy, do not

worry about paying your bills. You bills will be there whether you worry or not. By worrying, you create more hardship for yourself. You have to trust that the money to pay your bills is available to you—and keep moving forward. Spending your time worrying about your bills just creates more of that same vibration of lack.

Also, do not hoard money. Hoarding money sends out the signal that "there is not enough, so I need to hoard it all for myself." Money is an energy field. In order to grow, it needs to keep moving.

We've talked a lot about the "don'ts." Now, let's talk about some "do's":

1. Be thankful for what you already have. If you are being thankful for what you do have, you are not focused on what you don't have.

2. Track your good. The universe is constantly bringing you good in unexpected ways. Start noticing when it shows up for you. Did a friend buy you lunch when you had planned on paying? Did you go to the store to buy that $100 dress you'd been wanting and saving for, and when you got there, the dress was only $75? Did you plan on paying the babysitter $30 for a night of babysitting, and the neighbor offered to do it for free?   These are all examples of the ways in which unexpected income shows up. If you start noticing it and tracking it, you will be amazed at the way the universe is constantly bringing it to you. The more you notice and celebrate your good, the more good will show up for you!

3. When others receive, be as happy for them as you would be for you. When you are happy about others' receiving, you raise the vibration of receiving in yourself.

4. Be clear in your mind about what you want. Getting clear about what you want eliminates mind clutter and therefore helps draw your desires to you.

5. Take time for yourself everyday.

6. Do things only because you want to, not out of guilt or obligation. If you don't want to do something, say no.

7. Set boundaries for yourself, and always follow through with them.

8. Remove clutter from your home.

9. Release your attachment to money so it can flow. Part of what keeps money from you is your attachment to it. Water is the very thing that nourishes you, yet you would think nothing of throwing half a glass of it down the drain, knowing that it will flow right back out of the faucet. Grasping on the value that you think money has actually keeps money from you. Let it flow by releasing the attachment.

10. Give. When you give money, you are contributing to the flow of the universe, knowing that it will flow back to you. In this game, giving and receiving are one and the same. Make sure that when you give, it is because you want to—not out of a sense of obligation. If you give with an open heart, the money keeps flowing. If you give with a closed heart, you block the flow.

11. Know that money isn't something that only other people have. It's something that you have.

12. Meditate daily. Meditating every day quiets the mind and helps you to be clear. It's hard to create with mind clutter.

13. No matter what your reality looks like, know that you are an abundant human being and keep moving forward. Do not let your reality distract you from what you know!

IN CLOSING

The information in this program can help you to create the life of your dreams. Start today! Make a list of the things that you would like to see show up in your life. Keep focusing on your list until every item is a part of your reality.

You now have the tools to start making positive changes in your life and moving in the direction of PROSPERITY. When you apply these principals, you can accomplish anything. Nothing can stop you now. Reach for the stars, and remember that you are transforming old beliefs, old thought patterns, and old lifestyles on your way to the abundance that you deserve.

There may be times on this journey when you feel as if you are not moving in the right direction, but do not become frustrated. Do not allow your doubt to overcome all the work you have done. Instead, keep your focus on the outcome you desire. Know that your current thoughts are creating your future. Be gentle on yourself. This is a way of life that you have been taught, and you are changing an entire belief system. Trust your knowing that this is the right direction at all times.

Remember that even when lightning strikes, causing a forest fire, and hundreds of trees are burned—that it is the divinity of nature making way for new seedlings that will grow the most amazing forest you have ever seen. Without that fire and what looks like a "disaster" to us, the new forest could never grow. You, too, are growing a new forest. The new seedlings are your future. If it starts to look like a fire is burning, in that moment of apparent "disaster," know that this is your sign that your old beliefs or "old trees" are burning away. This experience is moving you to the beauty of your new forest and to the life that <u>you deserve</u>.

Bagua Map

Many thanks to all that have purchased my book. My wish for you is that you find all of the prosperity that you deserve through these concepts. I feel I am very fortunate to have been able to experience these life lessons and that I am now able to share them with you. Best wishes on your journey.

Julie Nichol

If you would like to purchase Feng Shui items, chakra-related products, other related products, or for personal intuitive consultations, please visit our website at:

www.connectwithyourtruth.com

Made in the USA
Lexington, KY
03 May 2013